Kaplan Publishing are constantly finding new ways to make a difference to your studies and our exciting online resources really do offer something different to students looking for exam success.

This book comes with free EN-gage online resources so that you can study anytime, anywhere.

Having purchased this book, you have access to the following online study materials:

CONTENT	ACCA (including FFA,FAB,FMA)		AAT		FIA (excluding FFA,FAB,FMA)	
	Text	Kit	Text	Kit	Text	Kit
iPaper version of the book	✓	✓	✓	✓	✓	✓
Interactive electronic version of the book	✓					
Fixed tests / progress tests with instant answers	✓		✓			
Mock assessments online			✓	✓		
Material updates	✓	✓	✓	✓	✓	✓
Latest official ACCA exam questions		✓				
Extra question assistance using the signpost icon*		✓				
Timed questions with an online tutor debrief using the clock icon*		✓				
Interim assessment including questions and answers		✓			✓	
Technical articles	✓	✓			✓	✓

* Excludes F1, F2, F3, FFA, FAB, FMA

How to access your online resources

Kaplan Financial students will already have a Kaplan EN-gage account and these extra resources will be available to you online. You do not need to register again, as this process was completed when you enrolled. If you are having problems accessing online materials, please ask your course administrator.

If you are already a registered Kaplan EN-gage user go to www.EN-gage.co.uk and log in. Select the 'add a book' feature and enter the ISBN number of this book and the unique pass key at the bottom of this card. Then click 'finished' or 'add another book'. You may add as many books as you have purchased from this screen.

If you purchased through Kaplan Flexible Learning or via the Ka... ...automatically receive an e-mail invitation to Kaplan EN·gage online. Please re... ...il to gain access to your content. If you do not receive the e-mail or book... ...exible Learning.

D1493086

If you are a new Kaplan EN-gage user register at www.EN-gage.c... ...the link contained in the email we sent you to activate your account. Then select the 'add a book' feature, enter the ISBN number of this book and the unique pass key at the bottom of this card. Then click 'finished' or 'add another book'.

Your Code and Information

This code can only be used once for the registration of one book online. This registration and your online content will expire when the final sittings for the examinations covered by this book have taken place. Please allow one hour from the time you submit your book details for us to process your request.

Please scratch the film to access your EN-gage code.

Please be aware that this code is case-sensitive and you will need to include the dashes within the passcode, but not when entering the ISBN. For further technical support, please visit www.EN-gage.co.uk

AQ2013 Level 3

Professional Ethics

REVISION KIT

KAPLAN
PUBLISHING

British Library Cataloguing-in-Publication Data

A catalogue record for this book is available from the British Library.

Published by:

Kaplan Publishing UK

Unit 2 The Business Centre

Molly Millar's Lane

Wokingham

Berkshire

RG41 2QZ

ISBN: 978-0-85732-898-4

© Kaplan Financial Limited, 2013

Printed and bound in Great Britain

CONTENTS

Features in this revision kit

In addition to providing a wide ranging bank of real exam style questions, we have also included in this kit:

- Paper specific information and advice on exam technique.

Our recommended approach to make your revision for this particular subject as effective as possible.

You will find a wealth of other resources to help you with your studies on the AAT website:

www.aat.org.uk

KAPLAN PUBLISHING

INDEX TO QUESTIONS AND ANSWERS

LEGAL CONSIDERATIONS – I

KAPLAN PUBLISHING

ASSESSMENT TECHNIQUE

- **Do not skip any of the material** in the syllabus.

- **Read each question** *very* carefully.

- **Double-check your answer** before committing yourself to it.

- Answer **every** question – if you do not know an answer to a multiple choice question or true/false question, you don't lose anything by guessing. Think carefully before you **guess**.

- If you are answering a multiple-choice question, **eliminate first those answers that you know are wrong**. Then choose the most appropriate answer from those that are left.

- **Don't panic** if you realise you've answered a question incorrectly. Getting one question wrong will not mean the difference between passing and failing

Computer-based exams – tips

- Do not attempt a CBA until you have **completed all study material** relating to it.

- On the AAT website there is a CBA demonstration. It is **ESSENTIAL** that you attempt this before your real CBA. You will become familiar with how to move around the CBA screens and the way that questions are formatted, increasing your confidence and speed in the actual exam.

- Be sure you understand how to use the **software** before you start the exam. If in doubt, ask the assessment centre staff to explain it to you.

- Questions are **displayed on the screen** and answers are entered using keyboard and mouse. At the end of the exam, you are given a certificate showing the result you have achieved.

- You need to be sure you **know how to answer questions** of this type before you sit the exam, through practice.

KAPLAN PUBLISHING

PAPER SPECIFIC INFORMATION

THE ASSESSMENT

FORMAT OF THE ASSESSMENT

There will be 9 tasks within the assessment.

- Five tasks will each require a more discursive response. These will be based on a scenario in a single accountancy practice but will each have different matters to be considered.

- Four tasks will be short answer questions and unrelated to that organisation.

Task	Learning outcome	Assessment criteria	Topics within task range
1	LO1	LO1.2, LO1.3	Legal, regulatory and ethical environment of the accounting and finance sector, including the role of professional bodies
2	LO1, LO2, LO3	LO1.6, LO2.1, LO2.6, LO3.2	Technical and professional competence and due care, and professional behaviour, including the scope of the accountant's work and the importance of working within range of professional expertise
3	LO2	LO2.4	Handling clients' money
4	LO2	LO2.5	Disclosure of confidential information
5	LO1, LO2	LO1.1, LO2.1	Fundamental principles of ethical behaviour and their application in the workplace
6	LO1, LO2	LO1.4, LO1.5, LO2.3	Organisational values and organisation/industry codes of practice and regulations, including why organisations and individuals should act in line with values and within both the law and relevant codes
7	LO2, LO3	LO2.2, LO3.5	Objectivity and the prevention and resolution of ethical conflicts and conflicts of interest
8	LO3	LO3.1, LO3.3, LO3.4	Taking appropriate action following suspected breaches of ethical codes and inappropriate or illegal behaviour by clients, colleagues or employers
9	LO2, LO4	LO2.3, LO4.1, LO4.2	Upholding sustainability and CSR in the public interest

Time allowed:

150 minutes (2½ hours)

PASS MARK:

The pass mark for all AAT CBAs is 70%.

 Always keep your eye on the clock and make sure you attempt all questions!

DETAILED SYLLABUS

The detailed syllabus and study guide written by the AAT can be found at:

www.aat.org.uk/

KAPLAN'S RECOMMENDED REVISION APPROACH

QUESTION PRACTICE IS THE KEY TO SUCCESS

Success in professional examinations relies upon you acquiring a firm grasp of the required knowledge at the tuition phase. In order to be able to do the questions, knowledge is essential.

However, the difference between success and failure often hinges on your exam technique on the day and making the most of the revision phase of your studies.

The **Kaplan textbook** is the starting point, designed to provide the underpinning knowledge to tackle all questions. However, in the revision phase, poring over text books is not the answer.

The **Kaplan workbook** helps you consolidate your knowledge and understanding and is a useful tool to check whether you can remember key topic areas.

Kaplan pocket notes are designed to help you quickly revise a topic area; however you then need to practise questions. There is a need to progress to exam style questions as soon as possible, and to tie your exam technique and technical knowledge together.

The importance of question practice cannot be over-emphasised.

The recommended approach below is designed by expert tutors in the field, in conjunction with their knowledge of the examiner and the specimen assessment.

You need to practise as many questions as possible in the time you have left.

OUR AIM

Our aim is to get you to the stage where you can attempt exam questions confidently, to time, in a closed book environment, with no supplementary help (i.e. to simulate the real examination experience).

Practising your exam technique is also vitally important for you to assess your progress and identify areas of weakness that may need more attention in the final run up to the examination.

In order to achieve this we recognise that initially you may feel the need to practice some questions with open book help.

Good exam technique is vital.

THE KAPLAN PETH REVISION PLAN

Stage 1: Assess areas of strengths and weaknesses

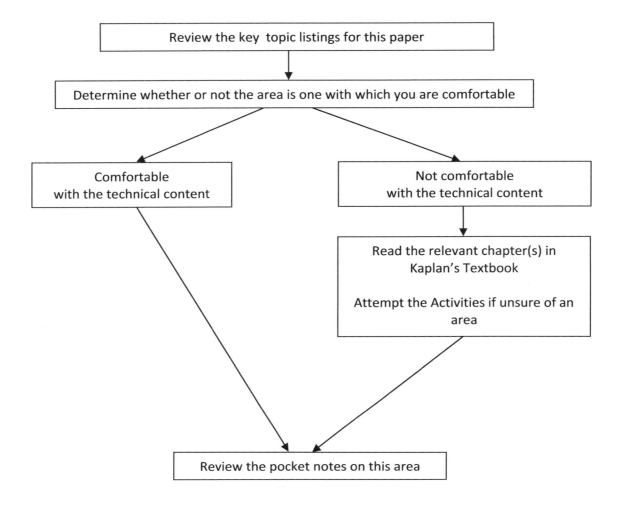

Stage 2: Practise questions

Follow the order of revision of topics as presented in this kit and attempt the questions in the order suggested.

Try to avoid referring to text books and notes and the model answer until you have completed your attempt.

Review your attempt with the model answer and assess how much of the answer you achieved.

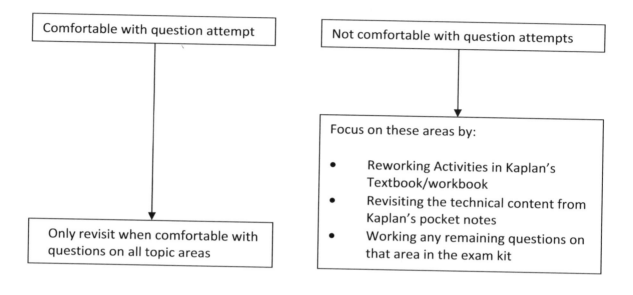

Stage 3: Final pre-exam revision

We recommend that you attempt at least one mock examination containing a set of previously unseen exam standard questions.

Attempt the mock CBP online in timed, closed book conditions to simulate the real exam experience

Section 1

PRACTICE QUESTIONS

ETHICS – THE PRINCIPLES

FUNDAMENTAL PRINCIPLES

1   JUST PRACTISING

Discuss whether the IFAC fundamental ethical principles are more (or less) relevant for accountants working in business compared to those in practice.

2   PRINCIPLES

Identify which ONE of the following options is NOT a fundamental principle in the IFAC code of ethics:

A   Objectivity

B   Confidentiality

C   Integrity

D   Honesty

3   OPTIONS

State which fundamental principles are defined as follows:

(a)   'The obligation on members to comply with relevant laws and regulations and avoid any action which may bring disrepute to the profession'.

(b)   'Members should be fair and not allow prejudice or bias or the influence of others to override professional or business judgements'.

(c)   'Refraining from disclosing outside the firm or employing the organisation's private information acquired as a result of professional and business relationships.'

4   DOUBLE OR QUITS

Professional accountants must maintain confidentiality in circumstances that give rise to a duty of confidentiality – for example, as a result of professional and business relationships.

State whether this is an ethical principle only, a legal obligation only, both or neither.

5 AAT

(a)   The IFAC approach to ethics is RULES / PRINCIPLES (delete as applicable) based.

(b)   IFAC's ethical guidance is designed to cover every ethical situation specifically, and prescribes exactly how you should respond.

State whether this statement is true or false.

6 FUNDA

Tick the appropriate column for each of the following.

Characteristic	Integrity	Objectivity
You are straightforward and honest		
You do not let your own bias or prejudice affect any decisions you make		
You follow all ethical guidelines		
You are independent of mind		

7 DUE CARE

The principle of professional competence and due care imposes certain obligations on professional accountants.

Which TWO options of the following are such obligations?

- To maintain professional knowledge and skill at the level required to ensure that clients or employers receive competent professional service

- To always know the answer to a question

- To be an expert on taxation

- To act diligently in accordance with applicable technical and professional standards

8 NIGHT OUT

Bella, a professional accountant, was invited on a 'night out' with others from the accounts department. This became quite a boisterous evening and it ended with the Finance Director removing a sign from the front of a shop which he brought into the office the next day as a reminder of the good evening.

(a)   State which fundamental ethical principle the Finance Director has breached.

(b)   State what course of action Bella should take.

9 INTEGRITY

Frankie is an AAT member working for Lightfoots Ltd as an assistant to the management accountant. His finance director has asked him to post a journal to transfer £20,000, a material sum, out of maintenance costs and into non-current assets, thus boosting profit. Frankie has checked the details and feels that there is no justification for the journal.

Explain what Frankie should do.

10 LAST

Jason is an AAT member in practice. The following matter arose this week:

Matter

One evening Jason had a drink with an old friend, Brian, an AAT member currently working as an accountant for a large manufacturing company.

Brian was extremely worried about events in the company he works for. He had been asked by one of the directors to become involved in an arrangement that would lead to personal financial gain for the director at the expense of the company. Brian had been offered financial reward for this, and it had been made clear to him that he would lose his job if he didn't comply.

(a)   State which ethical principle Brian has already breached by talking about this situation?

(b)   Explain what course of action is most appropriate for Brian to take immediately.

(c)   If the situation cannot be resolved via internal action, explain what Brian should do.

11 BEVIS

Bevis, an AAT member, has just joined a building company as a management accountant, after working for some years in a local accountancy practice.

The following situations have arisen in Bevis' first week at work.

Matter 1

When he first joined the company the Managing Director invited him out to lunch so that they could get to know each other. The Managing Director spent most of the time questioning Bevis about competitors who were clients of the firm Bevis used to work for.

Matter 2

As part of Bevis' work he needed to find out some information on behalf of the customer. When Bevis made the necessary phone call Bevis was told that the organisation did not have authority from the customer to disclose the information. When Bevis told his boss he told Bevis to ring back and pretend to be the customer.

Explain what should Bevis do in respect of the two matters above.

12 DILEMMA

Your boss has told you that there are going to be some redundancies in the company. You will not be affected, but he has named a number of people who will be, including a good friend of yours who is in the process of buying a holiday home in Cornwall. You know that your friend would not be able to afford the property if she were to lose her job and that she would pull out of the purchase if she knew about the redundancy plans.

The news of the redundancies will not be made public for several weeks.

(a)   State which fundamental ethical principle is primarily involved here.

(b)   Assess the ethical argument that you should tell your friend about the redundancies on the grounds it could save her unnecessary financial problems and distress.

13 SIMA

You are approached by your colleague Sima, who has received a complaint from a client (1) because she has not been able to produce a promised report on time (2). Sima says that this is because there is a new software system that she has not got to grips with yet (3), because she could not make it to the training event (4). Sima would like you to contact the client to tell them that there has been a problem with the system (5). She tells you more than you wish to know (6) about the background to the client's request. Office practice is for this type of report to be checked by a colleague before being sent out. Sima says that she has checked her own report, but asks you to sign it off without looking at it (7). You and Sima are friends and so you want to help (8). She also offers to buy you a drink (9) if you help. She also tells you not to tell anyone in case she gets into trouble (10).

(a) State which of the actions in the case study compromise integrity.

(b) State which of the actions in the case study compromise objectivity.

(c) State which of the actions in the case study compromise professional competence and due care.

(d) State which of the actions in the case study compromise confidentiality.

(e) State which of the actions in the case study compromise professional behaviour.

14 BENEFITS

Jacqui has recently been appointed as the chief accountant for a small public sector organisation. The other members of the senior management team (SMT) are very pleased with her appointment as they have really struggled to attract, recruit and retain good staff.

At the last meeting of the SMT it was decided that the benefits package for senior staff (including the SMT) was inadequate and that it needed revising.

Jacqui was asked to draw up the new package and, after considerable research and benchmarking, has decided that a significant increase is needed in the benefits package.

(a) Discuss which ethical principles are potentially compromised here.

(b) Identify which factors Jacqui should consider before making a decision what to do.

(c) Explain what the best course of action would be.

THREATS AND SAFEGUARDS

15 SUSHIL

Sushil is a member in business. His manager has asked him to falsify the accounts and has made it clear that if he refuses then he will lose his job.

(a) State which type of threat this situation represents.

(b) Explain what the best course of action would be.

16 INDEP

In order to maintain their independence accountants must ensure they have safeguards against independence threats.

Complete the following table to show which of the following are or are not threats.

	Threat	Not a threat
• Selfishness		
• Self review		
• Self interest		
• Honesty		
• Intimidation		

17 ALLSORTS

(a) Identify which ONE of these situations could result in an advocacy threat.

A Being present at a client's product launch

B Providing a mortgage company with details of your clients recent accounts

C Producing a client's management accounts as well as providing tax advice

D Being provided with lunch whilst at a client's offices for a meeting regarding a potential merger with an international company

(b) Identify which ONE of the following is an acceptable response to an intimidation threat.

A Doing nothing

B Contacting the police

C Reporting the matter to the Serious Organised Crime Agency

D Removing yourself from the situation creating the threat

18 JUSTIN

Justin is an AAT member in practice at Tipling LLP. He is a senior on an assurance assignment for Brittle plc.

He inherits a 10% shareholding in this client.

(a) Which type of threat does this situation represent?

(b) What would Justin's best course of action be?

19 JULIE

Julie has audited the accounts of Believe It plc as part of the assurance team for the past five years. She has been approached by Believe It plc with an offer of the Senior Accountant role.

(a) State which type of threat this situation represent.

(b) Suggest TWO safeguards the assurance firm should have in place concerning such a threat.

20   CPD

Answer the following question by selecting the appropriate options

(a)   Safeguards are controls that mitigate or eliminate threats to independence. TRUE/FALSE.

(b)   Identify which TWO of the following would be viewed by the AAT as examples of safeguards?

- A mission statement
- Ethical professional standards
- Disciplinary procedures

21   THREATS

For each of the following scenarios, state which type of threat is involved.

(a)   A practitioner acts on behalf of an assurance client in litigation or in resolving disputes with third parties.

(b)   A practice prepared the financial statements for a client and then also audited them.

(c)   A partner of an assurance engagement had been long associated with his client.

22   SAFE

Safeguards that may eliminate or reduce threats to objectivity to an acceptable level fall into two broad categories:

State the TWO broad categories of safeguards detailed in the AAT's Code of Professional Ethics.

23   GUARDS

In order to maintain their independence an accountant must ensure they have safeguards against independence threats.

Complete the following table to show which of the following are or are not safeguards.

	Yes, a safeguard	No, not a safeguard
• Door locks and bolts		
• Professional standards		
• Disciplinary procedures		
• Continuing professional development		

24   SAFE AND SOUND

Lara is a professional accountant in practice. Detailed below are three matters that have arisen with respect to some of Lara's clients.

For each of the situations below, identify the ethical threat to the client and recommend an ethical safeguard, explaining why that safeguard is appropriate.

Matter A

The director of Company W, a listed company, sold a substantial shareholding prior to the announcement of worse than expected results for the company.

Matter B

Mike is CEO of Company X and is also a non-executive director of Company Y and sits on the remuneration committee of that company.

Graham is CEO of Company Y and is also a non-executive director of Company X and sits on the remuneration committee of that company.

Mike and Graham are good friends and play golf together every Saturday.

Matter C

The chairman of Company Z does not like conflict on the board.

When a new director is appointed, the chairman always ensures that the director's family members obtain highly paid jobs in the company and, in the case of children, that they are sponsored by Company Z through college.

Company Z is very profitable, although the board appears to be ineffective in querying the actions of the chairman.

25   IN-HOUSE CODE

The directors of John Groom Ltd, a small manufacturing company, have drafted an ethical code for use within the organisation, based on ones used by competitors and the industry trade organisation. The Board also plan to encourage suppliers to adopt the code.

What is the legal status of this code?

PROFESSIONAL CONSIDERATIONS

THE ACCOUNTANCY PROFESSION

26   BEHAVE

A profession is distinguished by certain characteristics.

Identify which of the following options is NOT a characteristic of the accounting profession:

- Mastery of a particular intellectual skill, acquired by training and education;

- Adherence by its members to a common code of values and conduct established by its administrating body

- The desire to make as much money as possible

- Acceptance of a duty to society as a whole

27 OBJ

Identify which of the following objectives the accountancy profession is committed to.

- Development of an ethical approach to work.
- To make the most money for their members as possible
- To maximise shareholders wealth

28 PUBLIC INTEREST

Define what is meant by the 'public interest' and explain why it is relevant to the professional accountant.

29 REGULATED ACTIVITIES

Explain what is meant by 'statutory regulated functions' and their significance to AAT members in the UK.

Give THREE examples of statutory regulated functions.

THE ROLE OF PROFESSIONAL BODIES

30 BEN

(a) State which part of the Financial Reporting Council has direct responsibility for safeguarding the public interest by ensuring proper standards of conduct are adhered to by members in the UK.

(b) "The role of IFAC is to protect the public interest."

State whether this statement is true or false.

31 ABC

(a) Describe the role of the Serious Organised Crime Agency (SOCA).

(b) Describe the role of the International Ethics Standards Board for Accountants (IESBA)

(c) Explain the purpose of the Data Protection Act.

32 FRC

(a) State the overall role of the Financial Reporting Council.

(b) State what legislation governs what a company can do with information it holds about you.

33 EXASB

Briefly outline how auditing standards are set in the UK and how this is different from the setting of international auditing standards.

34   BODIES

(a)   State which professional accountancy bodies are a member of The Consultative Committee of Accountancy Bodies (CCAB).

(b)   State which professional accountancy bodies sponsor the AAT.

35   SPON

Answer the following questions by selecting the appropriate option in each case.

(a)   State which of the following is NOT a sponsoring body of the AAT.

ICAEW	ICAS	FRC	CIMA

(b)   State which of the following IS a sponsoring body of the AAT.

CAI	ACCA	IFAC	CIPFA

(c)   The role of IFAC is to protect the public interest by developing high quality international standards, promoting strong ethical values and encouraging quality practice.

TRUE/FALSE

KEEPING UP TO DATE

36   REDDIT

State which fundamental principle is safeguarded by keeping knowledge up to date and undertaking CPD.

37   KUP

State FOUR ways an accountant can ensure that their technical knowledge is kept up-to-date.

38   CYCLE

Mthbe is a professional accountant with his own small practice. He performs accountancy and tax services for a wide range of small clients including many sole traders.

(a)   Explain, with justification, TWO areas in which Mthbe needs to keep his technical knowledge up-to-date.

(b)   According to the AAT CPD policy how often should Mthbe complete a CPD Cycle?

(c)   How many stages does the AAT's CPD cycle have?

39   DEVELOPMENT

State which of the following options is NOT a stage in the CPD cycle.

- Evaluate

- Conduct

- Plan

- Assess

DISCIPLINARY PROCEDURES

40 PRO

Complete the following sentences using ONE of the options given.

(a) The principle of professional behaviour imposes an obligation on members to comply with relevant laws and regulations and avoid any action that may bring.......................

- scandal to the company
- personal financial loss
- disrepute to the profession

(b) The AAT state that any action taken by a member that adversely affects the AAT's reputation is grounds for...............

- disciplinary procedure
- legal proceedings
- disqualification

41 DISCIPLINE

A member is found to have acted in a way that adversely reflects the reputation of the association.

Identify, from the list below, the term that best describes the grounds for disciplinary action:

- Misconduct
- Misadventure
- Mistakes

42 PROCEDURE

(a) Ye Lin, a member in practice, is working for a company that is now under investigation for corruption. The Finance Director has told Ye Lin not to cooperate with the investigation team.

State whether Ye Lin should cooperate with the investigation or obey the FD.

(b) State what Ye Lin could be found guilty if she fails to cooperate with the investigation.

43 ACTION

Identify which of the following is NOT a disciplinary action that the AAT could apply in the case of a full or fellow member of the AAT.

- Be expelled from the Association
- Have his/her membership of the Association suspended
- Have a custodial sentence imposed
- Have his/her practicing licence withdrawn

LEGAL CONSIDERATIONS – I

CIVIL AND CRIMINAL LAW

44   CIVILISATION

State THREE differences between civil and criminal law.

45   AIMEE

(a)   State whether or not the AAT Code of Professional Ethics is an example of criminal law, civil law or neither.

(b)   Members should encourage an ethics-based culture in the workplace which emphasises the importance that senior management places on ethical behaviour.

What would be the best way to action this?

(c)   What is the role of the Financial Reporting Council?

46   PROOF

What is the normal burden of proof placed upon the prosecution in a criminal case?

A   Balance of probabilities

B   Beyond any doubt

C   Beyond reasonable doubt

47   DISPUTE

Jeremy is a professional accountant in business.

Jeremy was ill recently but still accepted new business from Frank. Unfortunately he did a poor job and made some significant miscalculations that have resulted in Frank receiving regulatory fines.

(a)   If Frank wishes to claim compensation from Jeremy, then which aspect of law would be involved – civil or criminal?

(b)   State TWO grounds upon which Frank could seek compensation.

MONEY LAUNDERING AND TERRORIST FINANCING

48   MATERIALITY

What is the minimum amount which is deemed immaterial for reporting money laundering?

49 MLRO

(a) Jeff, a member in practice has recently come across what he believes is an investigation by the regulatory authorities into allegations of money laundering at a large client.

He decides to communicate this to the Finance Director of the client.

State what offence Jeff will commit if he does this.

(b) What is the maximum sentence that Jeff can receive if found guilty of the offence

(c) Jeff's defence includes the claim that his organisation does not have a MLRO (Money Laundering Reporting Officer). In the absence of an MLRO, who should Jeff have approached with his concerns?

(d) A second part of Jeff's defence is that the amount in question was only £3,000 and that this is below the *de minimis* limit.

What is the *de minimis* limit?

50 OFFICIAL

The procedure for reporting known or suspected money laundering is to first internally report to the firm's MLRO. What does MLRO stand for?

- The Money Laundering Regulations Officer

- The Money Laundering Reporting Officer

- The Money Laundering Recording Officer

51 OMAR

Omar is a MLRO with L partnerships, a large accountancy practice. He has been told by an employee of suspected money laundering activity by a client of the practice.

What should Omar do next?

52 MONEY

Complete the following sentence by filling in the blank:

An offence is committed by an individual in the regulated sector if he fails to report where he has knowledge, _____ or reasonable grounds for suspecting money laundering activity.

53 DAVID

David, a member in practice, wishes to enter into a professional relationship with a client which will certainly last for a minimum period of two years.

(a) Outline THREE actions David must undertake as part of his customer due diligence process.

(b) Outline TWO factors members in practice must take into account when assessing the risk of their services being used to facilitate money laundering or terrorist financing.

54 ADAM

Adam, an AAT member within the UK, works for a firm of accountants, LOFT and Co, with a range of clients.

Matter 1

Adam has found an error in a client's tax affairs. The client has refused to disclose this known error, even after Adam has given notice of this error and an appropriate amount of time has been allowed to take action.

State to whom Adam is obliged to report this refusal to and the information surrounding it.

Matter 2

LOFT and Co recently billed a client, H Ltd, £5,000 and were very surprised when they received a cheque for £50,000 in settlement of the invoice. The Finance Director of H Ltd explained that it was a mistake on his part but asked whether LOFT and Co could send a cheque for the overpayment of £45,000 to Q Ltd, a different company and not one of LOFT's clients.

Discuss whether or not LOFT and Co should agree to the payment.

55 SAR

Answer the following question by selecting the appropriate options.

(a)   Which of the following are Money Laundering offences?

- Concealing, disguising converting or removing criminal property from the UK
- Entering into an arrangement which an individual knows facilitates the acquisition, retention or use of criminal property
- Entering into an arrangement which an individual suspects facilitates the acquisition, retention or use of criminal property

(b)   What does MLRO stand for?

(c)   What is an SAR?

56 BELLA

Bella is a MLRO for a large accountancy practice.

She has been informed of suspected money laundering by a large client, so must complete a suspicious activity report.

(a)   Which of the following, if any, must be included in a suspicious activity report?

- The identity of the suspect (if known)
- The amount of money involved (if known)
- The whereabouts of the laundered property (if known)

(b)   Bella is really busy at work at the moment and had therefore forgotten to submit the SAR. Has she committed an offence?

57 TIP TOP

Define 'tipping off'.

58 ROHINDER

Rohinder is an AAT member on an assurance engagement at Poster Plc. During the course of the engagement he hears that the client to about to be investigated by SOCA. Rohinder discusses this information with the Financial Director of Poster plc.

What offence has Rohinder potentially committed?

59 DUE

(a)   Which of the following is/are included within customer due diligence?

A   Making sure that your client is hard working

B   Verifying your client's identity

C   Checking that your client will pay his bills

(b)   Customer due diligence is performed to comply with

A   Companies Act 2006

B   Money laundering legislation

C   AAT ethical guidance

WHISTLEBLOWING

60 DISMISS

Sarah, a member employed in a division of a large building company, believes that one of the contract managers is attempting to short cut building regulations by using substandard building materials in a new school.

Sarah has spoken to an internal whistle-blowing helpline about the situation and now the divisional manager is threatening to have her dismissed "for not being a team player".

Explain whether or not Sarah is protected by the PIDA (1998)?

61 BLOW

To which TWO of the following disclosures does the Public Information Disclosure Act extend?

•   Endangerment of an individual's health and safety

•   Breach of contract

•   Breach of environmental legislation

62 CECILY

Cecily, an AAT member working for a large oil company has discovered a significant lapse in internal control procedures.

Explain what action Cecily should take.

63 WHISTLE

Explain what is meant by a 'qualifying disclosure' in the context of whistleblowing.

LEGAL CONSIDERATIONS – II

THE UK BRIBERY ACT (2010)

64   OFFENCE

Explain what is meant by bribery and outline the four offences detailed in the UK Bribery Act 2010.

65   DEFENCE

Explain the defences a commercial organisation could offer to a charge of bribery.

66   BRIBERY

Sarah works for a firm of accountants called B & Sons LLP and has recently introduced a new client to the firm called Leigh Davis. She has also been appointed as the audit manager for the client's company A Tours Limited which specialises in luxury holidays in the Caribbean. Leigh Davis was keen for Sarah to be appointed the audit manager for his company as he has known Sarah for a long time. He has recently offered Sarah free holidays in the Caribbean in return for her not asking questions about some irregularities in his company's financial statements.

Analyse the above scenario from the perspective of the law relating bribery. In particular, explain which criminal offences the various parties have committed or are at risk of committing.

67   NO DEFENCE

M plc is a large UK-based building firm that specialises in public sector contracts such as schools, hospitals and sports facilities.

Having a strong green and ethical reputation is vital to M plc's chances of winning government contracts. To protect its reputation, M has an internal ethics hotline for employees to raise any concerns they might have or evidence of wrongdoing.

Ever since the economic downturn in 2008, M plc has seen a major decline in its European business so the Board are keen to expand in other parts of the world.

Matter

In 2013 M plc was successful in winning a major contract to build new hospitals in Country H in Africa. However, a month later, the ethics hotline received a call concerning Mr Igbinadola, the agent who represented M plc in the negotiations with the government. The call claimed that Mr Igbinadola is well known for his excessive gifts and hospitality and paid for the MP involved in the negotiations to go on a lavish holiday just weeks before the contract was awarded.

The Board of M plc claims no knowledge of such gifts and are adamant they didn't authorise this.

Required

Discuss whether M plc could be guilty of an offence under the UK Bribery Act 2010.

THE FRAUD ACT (2006)

68 FRAUD

Answer the following questions by selecting the appropriate option in each case.

(a) Which of the following statements is true?

- Fraud is an honest mistake

- Error is deliberate falsification

- Fraud is committed with intent

(b) The risk of fraud can be evaluated by considering

- How much trouble you will get into if your boss finds out

- How the press will report the fraud

- Probability of fraud × size of resultant loss

(c) Which of the following is the most effective method of managing fraud?

- Fraud prevention

- Fraud detection

69 POLICE

Jack, an AAT member in practice, has recently undertaken an assignment to produce a set of accounts for a new client, and was paid for his time and expertise.

During the assignment Jack made a mistake that resulted in the client failing to win a significant contract, which in turn meant that the client's business could no longer continue.

Jack has now been advised that the business owner has contacted the police regarding the matter and has made a complaint of fraud.

Discuss whether Jack has committed fraud.

70 MAL

Which of the following are examples of employee malfeasance or misconduct?

(i) Employees submitting false expense claims

(ii) Managers falsifying health & safety paperwork

(iii) A sales manager deliberately overstating the benefits of a product

(iv) One employee clocking a colleague in and out of the building even when he is absent.

71 TRUE

Naill is an AAT member working for a large building company. The finance director has asked him to adjust some of the sales figures, so that the numbers look better than they actually are.

(a) Discuss whether Naill should do as the Finance Director instructs?

(b) Explain what is mean by 'false accounting'.

72   REFERENCE

Steve is a professional accountant working in practice.

Matter

Kept Ltd is Steve's oldest client and as well as the usual accountancy and tax services, Steve has recently been asked to write a reference to a new landlord confirming that Kept Ltd is likely to be able to pay its rent for the next 3 years.

While this would normally not be a problem, Steve is aware that Kept Ltd has been experiencing financial difficulties over the last 6 months, so he is wary of writing such a reference. To reassure him, the Chief accountant has offered to pay Steve a large fee for supplying the reference and suggested Steve should include a disclaimer of liability.

(a)   Analyse Steve's dilemma from an ethical point of view.

(b)   If Steve writes the reference, knowing Kept Ltd may not be able to pay, what crime is he potentially committing?

(c)   What difference would it make if Steve included a disclaimer of liability in the written reference?

THE DATA PROTECTION ACT (1998)

73   MIGUEL

Miguel's employer has shared his personal details with a market research agency. This breaches the employer's obligations under which of the following?

A   Data Protection Act

B   Confidentiality Stipulation Agenda

C   Disability Discrimination Act

74   DPA

Subject to certain exemptions, under the Date Protection Act (1998) all users of computers who are intending to hold personal data are required to register and supply relevant details.

(a)   State TWO exemptions to the DPA

(b)   State THREE of the details that the Act states should be supplied.

75   SECRET

Petra has encountered two matters where she feels the Data Protection Act is relevant:

Matter 1

She wants to request her personal credit report from a credit file company for free, using data protection legislation.

Matter 2

She receives a large amount of unsolicited (junk) mail. Using the Data Protection Act, she wishes to have these marketing activities blocked.

Comment on the relevance of the Data Protection Act to both of the above scenarios.

OTHER RELEVANT REGULATION

76 REG

Answer the following questions by selecting the appropriate option in each case.

(a) Health and safety compliance is governed by which of the following?

A   Employment law

B   Your specific contract with your employer

C   Discrimination law

(b) Which of the following is NOT restricted by discrimination legislation?

A   Employing only strong men who are more useful around the place

B   Employing only attractive women because clients like it that way

C   Sacking somebody who has stolen money from the company

77 LTD

(a) Whilst working for a company, you may learn important and confidential information. It is against the law, to buy or sell shares in any company based on private, confidential information.

What is this offence known as?

(b) The Data protection act is only applicable to publicly listed companies – true or false?

THE ACCOUNTANT IN PRACTICE

ACCEPTING WORK

78 CHRIS

(a) Chris, a member in practice, performs services for both Yin Ltd & Yang Ltd. Yin Ltd is currently considering a takeover of Yang Ltd.

State which fundamental principle is at threat for Chris.

(b) Simon, a member in practise, inherits from his Grandfather shares in a company that his firm audits.

State which threat this situation represents and outline what Simon's best course of action is.

79 DENT

(a) Fill in the missing words in the following statement:

The AAT guidelines on professional ethics that you should be independent in................. and ....

(b) A client has asked Mo for advice on corporation tax. Mo studied corporation tax two years ago but has never performed any real tax work before. What should Mo do?

80   DILIGENCE

Conner, a member in practice, has just received a call from a potential new client asking Conner to help in a business transaction. However when asked for his address, the client said he would rather not say.

(a)   Advise Conner on how to respond to the client.

(b)   Explain what other action(s) Conner should take.

81   JESS

(a)   Jessica, a member in practice, has been tasked to complete an important assignment. However, she knows that she will not have enough time complete the work properly

State which fundamental principle is at threat.

(b)   Beverley, a qualified AAT member in practice, has been asked to complete a tax assignment involving some complex Inheritance Tax calculations, which Beverley does not feel confident she fully understands.

Explain whether or not Beverley should undertake the assignment.

HANDLING CLIENT MONIES

82   LIMIT

(a)   Keely, a member in practice, is unsure of what exactly to do with a Client's money that she has been asked to keep custody of for a year.

What should Keely do?

(b)   Suppose Keely takes custody of the money and places it into a separate account and, over the course of the year, £500 interest is accrued on the account.

Can Keely keep the £500?

83   KAI

Kai, is a member in practice. His client has entrusted him to hold £2,000 on his behalf.

When Kai completed the Client's accounts last month he took £300 full payment for work completed, directly from the Clients account.

The client has just telephoned Kai after finding out his account has been debited and accused Kai of stealing.

Explain whether or not Kai should have taken the money.

84   ACCEPTANCE

Recommend 5 activities that should adopted when accepting to hold money on behalf of a client.

DEALING WITH INAPPROPRIATE CLIENT BEHAVIOUR

85   MEERA

Meera works for a large accountancy firm as a tax specialist. Recently two matters have arisen:

Matter 1

On Monday Meera was in a meeting with a potential new client.

The potential client started by stating that he felt Meera's fees proposal was far too high and she needed to reduce them substantially.

He then said that he believed his tax bill for the previous year was also too high but if Meera guaranteed to reduce his tax bill, then he would come to her firm.

Meera had a quick look at the figures and she believed the sum looked reasonable.

(a)   Explain what Meera should do in response to the client's requests

Matter 2

On Tuesday Meera had a dispute with Greg, is a new client. After analysing Greg's tax affairs Meera had found a material error in the previous year's tax return that resulted in an underpayment of tax. The previous tax computations were prepared by Greg's previous accountant,.

Meera advised Greg to tell HMRC about the error but so far he has refused to do so, claiming it is "their problem, not his".

(b)   Should Meera tell HRMC about the error?

(c)   What should Meera do if Greg continues to refuse to inform the HMRC?

86   DONNA

Donna, an accountant in practice, has recently been working on the tax computations for a client, Stoppard plc.

In preparing this year's tax returns Donna realised that she made an error preparing the last tax returns which resulted in an underpayment. She told the Finance Director of Stoppard plc about the error but he is refusing to tell the HMRC, claiming "she made the mistake, not him".

What should Donna do?

CONFIDENTIALITY AND DISCLOSURE REVISITED

87 SARAH

Sarah is an AAT member working for a small accountancy practice.

She has received a call from a property agent asking for the following information about a client.

- Accounts for the previous three years

- An assurance that they will be able to meet the rent for a proposed property rental

    (a)   Advise Sarah on the appropriate course of action, with regards to giving the agent the Accounts for the previous three years.

    (b)   Advise Sarah on the appropriate course of action, with regards to giving the agent an assurance the client will be able to pay.

88 SUCCESS

In which of the following circumstances is it acceptable to breach confidentiality, in respect of Directors Remuneration?

- When by a member of the clients staff who is not involved in the payroll function

- When by a friend who is a member of the clients' staff involved in the preparation of the monthly management accounts

- When asked by a member of the clients production staff

- None of the above

89 DUMPING

During your lunch you read an article in the FT about a case where a company was prosecuted through the courts for a breach of environmental laws regarding the dumping of toxic waste into drains, which subsequently lead to the open ocean. The case included testimony from the company's auditors which secured the prosecution. You discuss this with one of the juniors who says that she thought that this would constitute a breach of confidentiality on behalf of the auditor.

Write a response to this comment.

OTHER CONSIDERATIONS

90 EDWARD

Edward, an AAT member, is just setting up his own accountancy practice. He wants to use adverts that emphasise that his firm is better than others in the area, and give offers of reduced rates for services.

Advise Edward.

91 MARKETING

Your firm is currently running a new marketing campaign. The following are ideas that the partners want to include in the campaign.

Review the quotes given and decide whether they are appropriate or not. If not explain why.

- 'Do you feel that your existing accountants are letting you down?'

- 'Better than the rest and cheap as chips'

- 'No hidden extras – the price we say is the price you pay'

- 'Recommend us to a friend and get a 15% discount on your audit fees'

- 'Introductory offer – half price tax returns'

SUSTAINABILITY

92 SUSTENANCE

Outline the roles of professional accountants in contributing to sustainability.

93 GREEN GAINS

Describe three ways in which an increased emphasis on sustainability can result in improved profits for a firm.

94 TIO RINO

Tio Rino is a global mining company that has received much criticism in the past over its sustainability record. Press coverage has focussed on environmental damage, pollution, labour and human rights abuses and deforestation as well as criticism that Tio Rino mines coal (which contributes to global warming when burnt) and uranium (which contributes to concerns over nuclear power).

However, on its website the firm states the following:

"Our business is *sustainably* finding, mining and processing mineral resources."

Suggest TWO ways for each of the Triple Bottom Line reporting headings that a mining company such as Tio Rino can be a *sustainable* mining company.

95   HOGGS FURNITURE

Jacob is a professional accountant working for Hoggs Furniture Ltd ("Hoggs"), a furniture manufacturer that supplies many high street retailers.

Matter

At the last management meeting it was announced that a major client of the company was threatening to terminate their contract with Hoggs unless it could demonstrate a clear commitment to sustainability.

The team were unclear what this meant for Hoggs and asked Jacob to investigate further.

Required

(a)   Explain what is meant by "sustainability".

(b)   Explain FOUR areas that Jacob should appraise in order to answer the client's concerns.

(c)   List THREE other ways Jacob can contribute to sustainability through his role as an accountant.

Section 2

ANSWERS TO PRACTICE QUESTIONS

ETHICS – THE PRINCIPLES

FUNDAMENTAL PRINCIPLES

1   JUST PRACTISING

Compliance with ethical principles is EQUALLY important for ALL accountants, whether in business or in practice.

This is because these are the fundamental principles of the profession even if how they are complied with may be different for accountants in different roles.

2   PRINCIPLES

Honesty, while implied by integrity, is NOT a fundamental principle in itself.

3   OPTIONS

A   Professional behaviour

B   Objectivity

C   Confidentiality

4   DOUBLE OR QUITS

Confidentiality is BOTH an ethical principle and a legal obligation.

5   AAT

(a)   The AAT's approach to ethics is a principles-based approach

(b)   False – the AAT's ethical code offers guidance rather than rules so the accountant must exercise judgement in applying the principles.

6   FUNDA

Characteristic	Integrity	Objectivity
• You are straight forward and honest	✓	
• You do not let your own bias or prejudice affect any decisions you make		✓
• You stick to the ethical guidance	✓	
• You are independent of mind		✓

7   DUE CARE

The principle of professional competence and due care imposes the following obligations on members:

To maintain professional knowledge and skill at the level required to ensure that clients or employers receive competent professional service.	✓
To act diligently in accordance with applicable technical and professional standards.	✓

8   NIGHT OUT

(a)   This situation displays a breach of Professional Behaviour.

(b)   Bella should suggest to the Finance Director that he should replace the sign, and possibly discuss the matter with the Managing Director.

9   INTEGRITY

Appropriate responses include the following:

Internal action

• Discuss the matter with the Finance Director to see if there is a valid case for posting this journal. From the information given, this seems unlikely.

External action

If the FD refuses to change the request and Frankie still feels uncomfortable, then he could

• Go to the company's auditors to discuss the matter

• Seek guidance from the AAT

Ultimately if the situation is not resolved, then he should consider resigning.

Note: The wrong answer here is to suggest that he should post the journal without question as the Finance director is his senior. This is NOT an appropriate action.

10   LAST

    (a)   This situation displays a breach of Confidentiality.

    (b)   Jason's friend, Brian, should talk to the director. (**note:** you could have answered that he should get advice without breaching confidentiality, say by ringing the AAT ethics helpline)

    (c)   Brian should resign and state the reason for the resignation. Then report the situation to the external regulators.

11   BEVIS

Matter 1

Bevis should NOT tell the Managing Director anything that would be considered "private information" as this would be a breach of confidentiality.

Matter 2

Bevis should tell the customer that he has been unable to gain the information. Pretending to be a customer lacks integrity and would not be acting professionally.

12   DILEMMA

    (a)   Confidentiality.

    (b)   You should not tell your friend about the redundancies as to do so would breach confidentiality

13   SIMA

    (a)   **Integrity** – When you are asked to contact the client to tell them that there has been a problem with the system, (5) you are, in effect, being asked to tell a lie. At the very least you would be being reckless with the truth of having checked it if you sign it off without looking at it (7).

    (b)   **Objectivity** – It may be a small inducement, but it is an inducement when Sima says there is a drink in it for you if you help (9). The fact that you and Sima are friends and so you want to help (8) might indicate that you are being influenced in your decision-making by familiarity.

    (c)   **Professional Competence and Due Care** – When Sima says she has not been able to produce a promised report on time (2), it is clear that she is not professionally competent, which is reinforced by the fact that she is not able to operate the new software system that she has not got to grips with yet (3).

    (d)   **Confidentiality** – Generally, you should not be party to more than you wish to know about the background to the client's request (6), but then there can be a duty to disclose to a regulatory body when she tells you not to tell anyone in case she gets into trouble (10).

    (e)   **Professional Behaviour** – There is normally an appropriate way in which a complaint from a client (1) should be dealt with, while there is a continuing duty to develop, not only core skills, but those needed to work effectively for clients. Sima has compromised this when she could not make it to the training event (4).

14 BENEFITS

(a) The ethical principles potentially affected are as follows:

Integrity – How will Jacqui manage her personal interest with the need to be true and fair?

Objectivity- How will Jacqui manage her personal interest in the benefits package with the need to remain unbiased and consider only the relevant facts?

Professional Competence and Due Care – Does Jacqui have all the necessary skills to draw up such a package?

Professional Behaviour – How should Jacqui proceed so as not to bring discredit herself and the accountancy profession?

It would be very easy for Jacqui's recommendations to appear biased, even if she has acted ethically.

(b) Jacqui should start by considering the following issues:

Identify relevant facts:

She should consider the organisation's policies, procedures and guidelines, accounting standards, best practices, code of ethics, applicable laws and regulations.

Is the information used for assessing the potential new benefits package independent? Who else has been involved in the proposal for the new benefits package?

Identify affected parties:

Key affected parties are Jacqui and the rest of the SMT. Other possible affected parties are employees, human resources, shareholders and financial backers.

Identify who should be involved in the resolution:

Jacqui should consider not just who should be involved, but also for what reason and timing of their involvement.

She could think about contacting the AAT for advice and guidance, or discuss the matter with trusted colleagues or someone from human resources.

(c) **Possible courses of action**

Before explaining her findings to the SMT, it may be advisable for Jacqui to tell the SMT how she approached the project and who else was involved, for example, human resources.

She should declare her conflict of interest and not vote on the proposal for the new benefits package.

It may be advisable to involve human resources or another independent party to present the findings to the SMT. During the presentation, she should demonstrate how her findings were arrived at and who else was involved in the project.

THREATS AND SAFEGUARDS

15 SUSHIL

(a) This situation presents an intimidation threat.

(b) The best course of action would be to speak to his employer and explain that it is illegal to falsify the accounts.

16 INDEP

Threat	Threat	Not an independence threat
• Selfishness		✓
• Self review	✓	
• Self interest	✓	
• Honesty		✓
• Intimidation	✓	

17 ALLSORTS

(a) Being present at a clients' product launch constitutes an advocacy threat

(b) An acceptable response would be to remove yourself from the situation creating the threat.

18 JUSTIN

(a) This situation presents a self-interest threat.

(b) The best course of action is to remove Justin from this assurance engagement.

19 JULIE

(a) This situation presents a self-interest threat.

(b) Two safeguards the assurance firm should have in place are:

- A policy requiring the immediate disclosure of such an offer of employment
- A policy requiring Julie to be removed from the assurance engagement.

20 CPD

(a) True, Safeguards are controls that mitigate or eliminate threats to independence.

(b) TWO examples of safeguards are:

Ethical professional standards.	✓
Disciplinary procedures.	✓

21 THREATS

(a) This situation presents an advocacy threat.

(b) This situation presents a self-review threat.

(c) This situation presents a familiarity threat.

22 SAFE

TWO broad categories of safeguards detailed in the AAT's guidelines are:

• Safeguards created by the profession, legislation or regulation

• Safeguards in the work environment

23 GUARDS

Safeguards	Yes, a safeguard	No, Not a safeguard
• Door locks and bolts		✓
• Professional standards	✓	
• Disciplinary procedures	✓	
• Continuing professional development	✓	

24 SAFE AND SOUND

Matter A

The ethical threat is basically one of self-interest.

The director is using price sensitive information to ensure that a loss is prevented by selling shares now rather than after the announcement of poor results for the company.

One ethical safeguard would be a professional code of conduct that requires directors to carry out their duties with integrity and therefore in the best interests of the shareholders. The director would recognise that selling the shares would start the share price falling already and this would not benefit the shareholders.

As a code it may not be effective – the director could argue that selling shares prior to the results was designed to warn shareholders of the imminent fall in share price and was, therefore, in their best interests.

An alternative course of action is to ban trading in shares a given number of weeks prior to the announcement of company results (as happens in the USA where directors are not allowed to sell shares during 'blackout periods'). This would be effective as share sales can be identified and the directors could incur a penalty for breach of legislation.

Matter B

The ethical threat appears to be a lack of independence and self-interest regarding the setting of remuneration for these directors.

Not only do they have common directorships, but they are also good friends. They could easily vote for higher than normal remuneration packages for each other on the remuneration committees knowing that the other director will reciprocate on the other remuneration committee.

In corporate governance terms, one ethical safeguard is to ban these cross-directorships.

The ban would be enforceable as the directors of companies must be stated in annual accounts, hence it would be easy to identify cross-directorships. The ban would also be effective as the conflict of interest would be removed.

In professional terms, the directors clearly have a conflict of interest. While their professional code of ethics may mention this precisely as an ethical threat, Graham and Mike should follow the spirit of the code and resign their non-executive directorships.

This again would remove the threat.

Matter C

There is a clear ethical threat to the directors of Company Z.

They appear to be being bribed so that they do not query the management style of the chairman. The threat is that the directors will simply accept the benefits given to them rather than try to run Company Z in the interests of the shareholders. It is clearly easy to accept that option.

Ethical safeguards are difficult to identify and their application depends primarily on the desire of the directors to take ethical actions. In overall terms, the chairman does not appear to be directly breaching ethical or governance codes. The main safeguard is therefore for the directors not to accept appointment as director to Company Z or resign from the board if already a director.

The director could attempt to get the matter discussed at board level, although it is unlikely the chairman would allow this. Taking any other action is in effect 'whistle blowing' on all the directors and has the negative impact that the director would also have to admit to receiving 'benefits' from the company.

25 IN-HOUSE CODE

The code is a voluntary one prepared by John Grooms Ltd for its own use.

It cannot insist on suppliers adopting it.

The code cannot be statutory since that would be created under legislation/regulation/case law and used by many companies.

PROFESSIONAL CONSIDERATIONS

THE ACCOUNTANCY PROFESSION

26 BEHAVE

The desire to make as much money as possible, is not an objective of the accounting profession.

27 OBJ

Yes – the accountancy profession as committed to the development of an ethical approach to work.

28   PUBLIC INTEREST

The public interest is defined as "the collective well being of the community of people and institutions the professional accountant serves".

It is relevant to the professional accountant because a distinguishing mark of a profession is acceptance of its responsibility to the public. The accountant's obligations and responsibilities extend beyond those to their employer and/or clients.

29   REGULATED ACTIVITIES

An AAT member is open to practice in areas such as final account preparation, internal audit, management accounts and tax advice. However, even if you are a member of the AAT, you may not perform "statutory regulated functions" in the UK unless appropriately authorised.

Such activities include the following:

- external audit of UK limited companies or other bodies that require a registered auditor

- activities regulated by the Financial Conduct Authority and/or Prudential Regulatory Authority including investment business and corporate finance advice to clients;

- insolvency practice in accordance with the provisions of the relevant insolvency legislation.

THE ROLE OF PROFESSIONAL BODIES

30   BEN

(a)   In the UK, the Conduct Committee has direct responsibility for safeguarding the public interest by ensuring proper standards of conduct are adhered to by members

(b)   True, the Monitoring Committee (previously known as the Financial Reporting Review Panel) makes enquiries into apparent differences from the accounting requirements of the Companies Act 2006 and the financial statements in the annual accounts of large companies and where necessary seeks remedial action.

31   ABC

(a)   The role of the UITF (Urgent issues task force) is to resolve unsatisfactory or conflicting interpretations of accounting standards.

(b)   The AAT's approach to ethics is a **principles** based approach.

(c)   The purpose of the Data Protection Act is to give individuals protection against misuse of their personal data.

32   FRC

(a)   The overall role of the Financial Reporting Council is to promote good financial reporting.

(b)   Data Protection Act governs what a company can do with information it holds.

33 EXASB

Internationally, the International Audit and Assurance Standards Board (IAASB), part of IFAC, issues International Standards on Auditing (ISAs).

In the UK, the FRC issues UK versions of these International Standards on Auditing to tailor them to specific UK issues and to comply with UK legislation (e.g. the Companies Act). The FRC Board are advised on this by the Audit and Assurance Council.

34 CCAB

(a) The members of the CCAB are ICAEW, ICAS, ICAI, ACCA and CIPFA

Note: CIMA is NOT a member, having resigned in 2011.

(b) The sponsoring bodies of the AAT are ICAEW, ICAS, CIMA and CIPFA

35 SPON

(a) FRC is NOT a sponsoring body of the AAT.

(b) CIPFA is a sponsoring body of the AAT

(c) True, The role of IFAC is to protect the public interest by developing high quality international standards, promoting strong ethical values and encouraging quality practice.

KEEPING UP TO DATE

36 REDDIT

Keeping up to date and CPD safeguard the fundamental principle of professional competence and due care.

37 KUP

Ways an accountant can ensure that their technical knowledge is kept up to date include the following:

- reading professional journals,

- enrolling on update courses,

- complying with continuing professional development (CPD) requirements

38 CYCLE

(a) Mthbe needs to keep up-to-date in the following areas (only TWO needed):

- tax legislation/compliance
- money laundering regulations
- accounting/reporting standards
- regulation of accounting

The reasons for this are as follows:

- They are important areas because clients are businesses, which must comply with requirement for accurate accounts preparation and tax returns
- Mthbe needs to ensure he is technically competent to undertake the work (fundamental principle of professional competence and due care)
- Mthbe needs to protect himself re money laundering.

(b) The AAT CPD policy asks Mthbe to update his skills twice a year.

(c) The AAT's CPD cycle has four stages.

39 DEVELOPMENT

"Conduct" is NOT a stage in the CPD cycle.

DISCIPLINARY PROCEDURES

40 PRO

(a) The principle of professional behaviour imposes an obligation on members to comply with relevant laws and regulations and avoid any action that may bring disrepute to the profession.

(b) Any action that adversely affects the AAT's reputation is grounds for disciplinary procedures.

41 DISCIPLINE

Misconduct is grounds for disciplinary action.

42 PROCEDURE

(a) Ye Lin must cooperative fully with the investigation.

(b) If Ye Lin fails to cooperate as an AAT member she could be found guilty of misconduct.

43 ACTION

Having a custodial sentence bestowed on AAT members is not within the remit of the AAT.

LEGAL CONSIDERATIONS – I

CIVIL AND CRIMINAL LAW

44   CIVILISATION

The main differences between civil and criminal law are as follows:

	Civil	Criminal
Description	Claim to enforce rights in a civil court by a claimant against a defendant	Prosecution for a breach of the law in a criminal court by the state against the accused
Purpose	To settle disputes between individuals and to provide remedies.	The enforcement of particular forms of behaviour by the state.
Burden of proof	Liability must be shown on the balance of probabilities (lower standard of proof)	Guilt must be shown beyond reasonable doubt (high standard of proof).
State Involvement	None	Acts as the prosecutor
Outcome	Compensation for the party who wins.	Punishment of the accused through imprisonment or a fine.

45   AIMEE

(a)   The AAT Guideline on Professional Ethics is NOT part of criminal law – for example, ethical misconduct can result in discipline but not custodial sentences

(b)   Introduce an official ethical code of practice, communicate this to all employees (with formal training if necessary) and ensure an example is set by senior management (establishing the "tone at the top").

(c)   The role of the Financial Reporting Council is to issue new accounting and auditing standards and amend existing ones.

46   PROOF

D

The standard of proof to be satisfied in civil actions, not criminal actions, is on a balance of probabilities. In criminal actions, the case must be proved beyond reasonable doubt. The words 'every' and 'any' are inappropriate for use.

47   DISPUTE

(a)   Compensation would be sought via a civil action rather than a criminal prosecution.

(b)   The most likely grounds upon which Frank could seek compensation would be breach of contract and/or negligence by Jeremy.

MONEY LAUNDERING AND TERRORIST FINANCING

48 MATERIALITY

There is no minimum amount for the reporting of money laundering

49 MLRO

(a) Jeff has just committed the offence of tipping off.

(b) The maximum sentence is 5 years.

(c) In the absence of an MLRO, Jeff should have approached SOCA with his concerns.

(d) De minimus means no minimum limit.

50 OFFICIAL

The procedure for reporting known or suspected money laundering is to first internally report to the Money Laundering Reporting Officer (MRLO).

51 OMAR

Omar should now complete a Suspicious Activity Report, which should be sent to SOCA.

52 MONEY

An offence is committed by an individual in the regulated sector if he fails to report where he has knowledge, *suspicion* or reasonable grounds for suspecting money laundering activity.

53 DAVID

(a) As part of his customer due diligence process, David must do the following:

- Verify the client's identity on the basis of documents, data or other reliable information

- Obtain evidence so he is satisfied that he knows who any beneficial owners are

- Obtain information on the purpose and intended nature of the client relationship

(b) Members in practice must assess the risk of their services being used to facilitate money laundering or terrorist financing, taking into account (1) the nature of the client and (2) the client's business.

54 ADAM

Matter 1

Adam is obliged to report this refusal to disclose and the information surrounding it to the firm's Money Laundering Reporting Officer (MLRO).

Matter 2

This scenario also gives grounds for suspicion of money laundering. Why doesn't the client, H Ltd, simply want LOFT to repay them and then it up to them whether they want to pay anything to Q Ltd? Is it to make funds difficult to trace, so "dirty cash" becomes a nice clean cheque from a reputable accounting firm?

Any overpayment by a customer should be thoroughly investigated by a senior member of finance function staff and only repaid to the customer once it has been established that it is right/legal to do so.

Similarly the request to pay a third party should be scrutinised before any payment is agreed to. Without further information the transaction does not make commercial sense.

Unless investigations satisfy any concerns raised, then LOFT should refuse the payment and the MRLO should fill in a Suspicious Activity Report (SAR) to be sent to SOCA.

55 SAR

(a) All are offences under term Money Laundering:

(b) MLRO stands for Money Laundering Reporting Officer.

(c) SAR stands for Suspicious Activity Report.

56 BELLA

(a) The suspicious activity report must include

- The identity of the suspect (if known).

- The whereabouts of the laundered property (if known).

(b) Yes, it is an offence not to submit a SAR in this situation

57 TIP TOP

Tipping off is defined as the legal term meaning to tell the potential offender of money laundering that the necessary authorities have been informed, or to disclose anything that might prejudice an investigation.

58 ROHINDER

Rohinder has potentially committed the offence of Tipping off.

59 DUE

(a) Customer due diligence processes includes verifying your client's identity.

(b) Customer due diligence is performed to comply with money laundering legislation.

WHISTLEBLOWING

60   DISMISS

The Public Interest Disclosure Act 1998 (PIDA) protects individuals from dismissal who disclose confidential information, whether internally or to a prescribed regulator when given in good faith.

Sarah is thus protected under the PIDA.

61   BLOW

(a)   The rights of employees who disclose confidential information are protected under which PIDA.

(b)   The PIDA covers the following disclosures

Endangerment of an individual's health and safety.	✓
Breach of ethical guidelines	✓

62   CECILY

Cecily should first discuss with her direct manger, and then if no resolution can be found notify the AAT.

63   WHISTLE

To define "whistle blowing" we consider that the following three essential elements are necessary

- The perception by someone within an organisation that something is morally amiss within that organisation.

- The communication to parties outside the organisation.

- The perception by at least some of those in authority in that organisation that outside communication ought not to have been made.

LEGAL CONSIDERATIONS – II

THE UK BRIBERY ACT (2010)

64 OFFENCE

Bribery is a crime under the Bribery Act 2010.

Bribery itself is defined as both the giving and receiving of bribes in terms of someone who facilitates, gives or receives an advantage (which is usually financial) in connection with a person performing a function improperly.

The Bribery Act 2010 creates four offences:

- bribing a person to induce or reward them to perform a relevant function improperly

- requesting, accepting or receiving a bribe as a reward for performing a relevant function improperly

- using a bribe to influence a foreign official to gain a business advantage

- a new form of corporate liability for failing to prevent bribery on behalf of a commercial organisation

65 DEFENCE

For a commercial organisation, it is a defence to have in place 'adequate procedures' to prevent bribery.

This may include implementing anti-bribery procedures.

It is important that firms consider what procedures are "adequate" for their firm given the risks they face and the way they run their business. The procedures should be proportionate to the risk posed.

For some firms there will be no need to put bribery prevention procedures in place as there is no risk of bribery on their behalf. Other firms may need to put measures in place in key areas, such as gifts and hospitality, as this is the area where they have identified a risk.

Corporate ignorance of individual wrongdoing will provide no protection against prosecution.

66 BRIBERY

The Bribery Act 2010 creates four offences:

1 bribing a person to induce or reward them to perform a relevant function improperly

2 requesting, accepting or receiving a bribe as a reward for performing a relevant function improperly

3 using a bribe to influence a foreign official to gain a business advantage

4 a new form of corporate liability for failing to prevent bribery on behalf of a commercial organisation

Leigh Davis is guilty of bribery (offence 1 above) under the Act as he is bribing Sarah by offering her free holidays in return for her performing her function as an audit manager improperly.

Sarah is guilty of receiving a bribe (offence 2 above) from Leigh Davis.

B & Sons LLP could also be guilty of bribery of the Act for failing to prevent bribery (offence 4 above) unless they can show that they had in place 'adequate procedures'.

Both Leigh and Sarah could receive a maximum jail sentence of up to ten years.

If B & Sons LLP is found guilty they could be liable for an unlimited fine.

67 NO DEFENCE

The Bribery Act 2010 creates four offences:

1   bribing a person to induce or reward them to perform a relevant function improperly

2   requesting, accepting or receiving a bribe as a reward for performing a relevant function improperly

3   using a bribe to influence a foreign official to gain a business advantage

4   a new form of corporate liability for failing to prevent bribery on behalf of a commercial organisation

Certainly the excessive nature of the hospitality would mean that it would be viewed as an attempt to bribe the MP concerned.

While M plc could argue that they are not guilty of 1, 2 and 3 above, they are likely to be found guilty under offence 4. Even though Mr Igbinadola was an agent and not an employee and even though the Board claim ignorance, the company could still be found guilty of failing to prevent bribery.

The only possible defence would be to demonstrate that they had adequate procedures in place to prevent bribery, but in this case it looks difficult to prove this.

THE FRAUD ACT (2006)

68 FRAUD

(a)   Fraud is committed with intent.

(b)   The risk of Fraud is governed by the probability of fraud × size of resultant loss.

(c)   Fraud prevention is the most effective method of dealing with Fraud

69 POLICE

Looking at the following pre-requisites of fraud:

- Motive – it is difficult to see why Jack would want the client's business to fail – there is no motive

- Dishonesty – there is no evidence that this is anything other than an honest mistake

In summary, no, Jack has not committed Fraud

70 MAL

All the examples given are examples of Employee Malfeasance

71 TRUE

(a) No, Naills as an AAT member has a duty to produce a true and fair view of the accounts.

(b) The definition of false accounting is concealing or falsifying accounting records with a view to personal gain or providing false information that is misleading or deceptive.

72 REFERENCE

(a) The ethical principles involved here are as follows:

- **Integrity** – Steve must be straightforward and honest in all professional and business relationships. Integrity also implies fair dealing and truthfulness and there is a danger that the reference is not a fair or true representation of the facts as he sees them.

- **Objectivity** – the large fee should not be allowed to colour Steve's judgement. This presents a self-interest threat.

  It could also be argued that, because Kept Ltd is Steve's oldest client, then there is also a familiarity threat to objectivity.

- **Professional behaviour** – writing a reference that Steve suspects to be false could bring discredit to himself and the profession.

(b) Steve is potentially guilty of "fraud by false representation" under the Fraud Act 2006. This is where a person makes "any representation as to fact or law ... express or implied" which they know to be untrue or misleading.

There is also the possibility that the large fee could be interpreted as a bribe under the Bribery Act 2010 and Steve could be found guilty of passive bribery (receiving a bribe) under the Act.

(c) It is acceptable practice for Steve to include a disclaimer of liability and it certainly does no harm to include one. However, disclaimers can be challenged in court so may not afford Steve any protection.

If he has serious doubts over whether or not Kept Ltd will be able to pay the rent, then he shouldn't write the reference.

THE DATA PROTECTION ACT (1998)

73 MIGUEL

(a) This breach's the employer's obligations under the Data Protection Act.

(b) Buildings are not an example of intellectual property

74   DPA

Under the Date protection act all users of computers who are intending to hold personal data are required to register and supply

- Name and address of data user.

- Description of, and purpose for which, data is held.

- Description of source data.

- Identification of persons to whom it is disclosed.

- Names and non UK countries to which transmission is desired.

- Name of persons responsible for dealing with data subject enquiries.

75   SECRET

Matter 1

The DPA is relevant here. The credit file company must provide Petra with access to her credit file. However, she does not have the right to request this for free and may have to pay a fee.

Matter 2

The DPA would give Petra the right to prevent information stored about her being processed for the purposes of direct marketing. However, junk mail is likely to be sent to a large number of recipients and therefore is not **direct** marketing.

OTHER RELEVANT REGULATION

76   REG

(a)   Health and safety compliance is governed by employment law.

(b)   Sacking somebody who has stolen money from the company is NOT discrimination.

77   LTD

(a)   To buy or sell shares in any company based on private, confidential information is the offence of Insider Trading.

(b)   False, the Data protection act is NOT only applicable to publicly listed companies.

THE ACCOUNTANT IN PRACTICE

ACCEPTING WORK

78   CHRIS

(a)   This situation represents a threat to the fundamental principle of confidentiality.

(b)   This situation represents a self Interest threat. Simon's best course of action is to sell the shares.

79   DENT

(a)   The AAT guidelines on professional ethics state that you should be independent in mind and appearance

(b)   Mo should not accept the engagement, as he is not competent to do so.

80   DILIGENCE

(a)   To comply with customer due diligence (part of money laundering regulations), the best course of action for Connor to take would be to inform the client that without knowing the correct address the client/accountant relationship cannot be forged.

(b)   The reluctance to disclose an address raises concerns over possible money laundering, so Connor must consider reporting the conversation to SOCA.

81   JESS

(a)   This situation represents a threat to the fundamental principle of Due Care.

(b)   No, Beverley should not undertake the task. This situation represents a threat to the fundamental principle of Technical Competency.

HANDLING CLIENT MONIES

82   LIMIT

(a)   At the very least, Keely should keep the money in a separate bank account.

(b)   No, Keely cannot keep the £500. To do so would constitute the crime of theft.

83   KAI

No, Kai should not have taken the money directly.

Kai should have only have transferred monies if the Client has given express permission to do so.

84   ACCEPTANCE

Choose 5 from:

- You must keep client money separately from any personal or firm money.

- Open a separate bank account for client money.

- Give written notice to the bank stating the title and nature of the account.

- Bank any client money without delay.

- Only release it on instruction from the client / use it for the purpose intended.

- Have full records and accounts for this money and a statement of the account given to the client at least once a year.

- If the client is giving you over £2000 for more than two months you should put it in an interest bearing account.

- Note that the interest belongs to the client and should be credited to their account.

DEALING WITH INAPPROPRIATE CLIENT BEHAVIOUR

85 MEERA

Matter 1

(a) **Fees**

While some discounting of fees is seen as commercially acceptable way to win business, heavily discounted fees are perceived as a "self interest" threat to professional behaviour. This does not mean that they should be avoided at all costs but guidelines need to be followed.

Fees should reflect the value of the professional services performed for the client and there is a risk with low fees of a perception that the quality of work could be impaired

Tax bill

Meera should consider the fundamental principle of Integrity.

It would be dishonest to promise to reduce a tax bill simply to gain a client when she believes the bill to be reasonable.

Matter 2

(b) Meera should continue to advise Greg to contact the HMRC but it would be a breach of confidentiality for her to do so without his express permission, which seems unlikely in this case.

(c) If Greg, after having had a reasonable time to reflect, does not correct the error, Meera should do the following:

- Inform Greg that she/her firm can no longer act for him because funds dishonestly retained after discovery of a tax error become criminal property so their retention amounts to money laundering by Greg.

- Make an internal report on the matter to her firm's MLRO.

86 DONNA

Funds dishonestly retained after discovery of a tax error become criminal property so their retention amounts to money laundering by Stoppard plc

As she is now aware of the error, Donna should report to SOCA that she suspects Stoppard plc of money laundering because it has refused to notify the matter to HMRC. She will be protected from a claim for breach of confidentiality when making this report.

Knowing she may have been involved in money laundering, Donna needs to make an authorised disclosure to SOCA which may help protect her from a charge that she herself, in making the error, was engaged in money laundering.

CONFIDENTIALITY AND DISCLOSURE REVISITED

87 SARAH

(a) Sarah should obtain authority from the client to give the financial information.

(b) It is not possible to give an assurance regarding the client ability to pay the rent.

88 SUCCESS

(a) The following are all ways to maintain your integrity

- Refusing gifts that might influence behaviour ✓

- Avoiding activities that could affect your ability to perform your duties ✓

- Avoiding conflicts of interest ✓

(b) It is not acceptable to breach confidentiality under any of the following circumstances:

- When by a member of the clients staff who is not involved in the payroll function ✓

- When by a friend who is a member of the clients' staff involved in the preparation of the monthly management accounts ✓

- When asked by a member of the clients production staff ✓

89 DUMPING

Members have a duty of confidentiality.

However, there are occasions where the accountant has a professional or legal duty to disclose the information and therefore the breach of confidentiality is permissible.

Environmental damage is one such instance.

OTHER CONSIDERATIONS

90 EDWARD

No, Edward should not continue with this course of action.

91 MARKETING

Are you being taken for a ride by your existing accountants?	Inappropriate – it calls the integrity of rival firms into question
We are the best & cheapest in our field	Inappropriate – too non-specific – best and cheapest at what?
No hidden fees – the price you're given is the price you pay	Appropriate
Introduce a friend – get 10% off your fees	Appropriate
Our gift to you – your first personal tax return – half price	Appropriate

SUSTAINABILITY

92 SUSTENANCE

The roles of professional accountants in contributing to sustainability include the following:

- Challenging conventional assumptions of doing business

- Redefining success

- Establishing appropriate performance targets

- Encouraging and rewarding the right behaviours

- Ensuring that information flows that support decisions, and which monitor and report performance, go beyond the traditional ways of thinking about economic success.

Being sustainable requires the organisation to take full account of its impact on the planet and its people.

93 GREEN GAINS

An increased emphasis on sustainability can result in improved profits for the following reasons:

- Potential cost savings – e.g. due to lower energy usage

- Short term gain in sales – e.g. if customers are influenced by sustainability-related labels on products

- Long term gain in sales – e.g. due to enhanced PR and reputation

- Better risk management – e.g. pre-empting changes in regulations may save compliance costs.

94 TIO RINO

Mining companies can try to be sustainable by adopting the following:

Social issues ("people")

- Provide a safe and healthy workplace for employees where their rights and dignity are respected

- Build enduring relationships with local communities and neighbours that demonstrate mutual respect, active partnership, and long-term commitment

- Improve safety record re accident, fatalities

- Develop health programmes for local communities – e.g. in respect of AIDS/HIV in some African countries

- Ensure that if communities need to be moved or relocated, that resettlement and compensation are generous and cultural heritage is not compromised

- Invest in people over the long term by fostering diversity, providing challenging and exciting work and development opportunities, and rewarding for performance

- Ensure post-mining land use is discussed with local communities and is consistent with their aims and needs.

Environmental issues ("planet")

- Wherever possible prevent – or otherwise minimise, mitigate and remediate – harmful effects of activities on the environment.

- Avoid developing sites where the risk to biodiversity is particularly high.

- Develop new ways to reduce emissions of dangerous gases such as SO_2 and NO_2

- Plant new trees elsewhere to replace ones felled for mining to ensure biodiversity

- Landscape and replant sites after mining has finished. Pay for species to be repopulated.

- Use offsetting schemes to compensate for emission of greenhouse gases (e.g. schemes to plant additional trees somewhere else)

- Develop ways to process waste to avoid polluting the surrounding water system

- Reducing energy usage by more efficient processes

- Recycle as much waste products as possible

Economic issues ("Profit")

- Pay taxes without finding loopholes to avoid them.

- Ensure local communities benefit in terms of employments and a share of overall profits

- Reinvest in local communities and projects rather than taking all profits back to the mining company's home country.

95 HOGGS FURNITURE

(a) Sustainable development is defined as "development that meets the needs of the present without compromising the ability of future generations to meet their own needs" *(The UN's Bruntland Report)*.

Sustainability is thus more than just looking at environmental concerns. It relates to the continuity of **economic**, **social** and **environmental** aspects of human society.

Another way of looking at this is that sustainable businesses offer products and services that fulfil society's needs while placing an equal emphasis on people, planet and profits.

(b) Areas that Jacob should appraise in order to answer the client's concerns include the following:

- Whether non-renewable hard woods are used in manufacture.

    The client would want reassurance that all materials are form renewable sources.

- The energy efficiency and level of emission of greenhouse gases due to the operation of the factory.

    While these cannot be eliminated altogether, the client would want to see evidence that Hoggs has taken steps to improve energy efficiency (e.g. thermal insulation, double glazing, installation of solar panels, etc) or uses carbon offset schemes.

- Treatment of staff.

  Sustainability is not just about environmental issues but also incorporates social (people) aspects. The client may want to know what Hoggs' record is concerning accidents, staff development, diversity, etc.

- Tax

  Economic sustainability includes factors such as whether the company is paying tax and so contributing to the local/national community.

(c) Other ways Jacob can contribute to sustainability through his role as an accountant include the following:

- Helping create an ethics-based culture in Hoggs

- By championing and promoting sustainability

- By highlighting the risks of not acting sustainably and draw attention to reputational and other ethical risks

- By incorporating targets and performance measures consistent with a Triple Bottom Line (TBL) approach.

Section 3

MOCK EXAM QUESTIONS

Instructions to candidates

The time allowed to complete this mock exam **is 2 hours and 30 minutes**

TASK 1 (8 MARKS)

(a) Explain whether money laundering regulations would be classified as civil law or criminal law.

(b) State the role of the Consultative Committee of Accountancy Bodies (CCAB).

(c) State TWO sponsoring bodies of the AAT.

(d) Gemma works in tax and audit.

    (i) Explain whether Gemma works in any 'statutory regulated functions' and the distinction between these and 'other functions'.

    (ii) Identify the professional accountancy bodies involved in issuing the auditing standards that Gemma will use.

TASK 2 (12 MARKS)

(a) Professional accountants are required to have an up-to-date technical knowledge. State to which ONE of the five fundamental ethical principles this acts as a safeguard.

(b) Describe TWO ways an accountant could meet his/her CPD requirements.

(c) The following definition described which fundamental principle

'A member must be straightforward and honest in all professional and business relationships.'

(d) Ben, a member working for a firm in practice, has been asked by a client to review some complex tax computations but he is unsure about this as it is many years since he studied tax. What should he do?

(e) Greg, a professional accountant in practice, has been approached by a client to write a reference to the client's bank to help them raise a loan. Greg has doubts whether the client has the financial strength in order to be able to repay the loan.

    (i) What ethical principles and/or legislation are relevant to Greg's decision whether to supply the reference?

    (ii) Should Greg supply the reference?

    (iii) Is it acceptable for Greg to include a disclaimer of liability in the written reference?

TASK 3 (5 MARKS)

Bob is a member in practice who works for Mel, Smith and Co.

Whilst in the office, Bob, a member in practice, takes a telephone call from a client. The client is going abroad for several months and wants to send Mel, Smith and Co a cheque of £9,000, so that when the client's tax bill becomes due, Mel, Smith and Co can pay HMRC directly.

(a)   Can Bob advise the client that Mel, Smith and Co is able to accept this cheque and pay HMRC when the tax becomes due?

(b)   Identify TWO measures Mel, Smith and Co must take if they agree to accept the cheque.

(c)   Identify TWO consequences for Mel, Smith and Co if the correct procedures are not followed.

TASK 4 (5 MARKS)

Seth is a member in practice who specialises in accounting and tax services for individuals and businesses engaged in farming and agriculture.

One evening Seth goes out for a meal and some drinks after work with other members of his team. After several drinks, Seth starts telling some strangers on the next table about some of his clients and how he has been able to help them.

(a)   In which THREE situations is it acceptable to break confidentiality?

(b)   Identify TWO organisations or bodies whose rules Seth may have breached in talking to the strangers.

TASK 5–9

Task 5-9 are based on the following project scenario and the six matters listed. Each task indicates which of the six specific matters is relevant to the task

Project scenario

Smith & Jones is a well established firm of accountants with 10 offices, 25 partners and 250 staff based in East Norland.

You are Tom, one of twelve part qualified accountants, working in a department at Smith & Jones head office. You report to Stephen, the team manager and one of ten fully qualified professional accountants in the department.

You spend the majority of your time in the office preparing client accounts, tax returns and ad-hoc requests from clients. You occasionally go out of the office to client premises to undertake audit work.

The firm's clients include the following:

*   Morris Haulage Ltd – a family run company that operates 50 lorries and transports good across the country

*   Briggs Ltd – a rapidly growing manufacturer of water purifiers

*   RFT Ltd – a holiday company that owns a range of properties around the country that it rents out as holiday lets.

Recently the following six matters have come to light

Matter 1

Tom is sent out with two colleagues to work on the audit of Morris Haulage Ltd.

On the first morning of the audit, the finance director of Morris Haulage Ltd, Tony, greets the audit team. Tony is very friendly and welcoming, and tells the team: 'Whenever you want, help yourself to a sandwich for lunch at the staff canteen. Tell them Tony will cover the costs. Oh and seeing you has just reminded me, I must pay last year's audit fee! What do we owe you – is it £10,000?'

Matter 2

Smith & Jones has recently been embarrassed following news stories that one of its student staff members allegedly shop lifted some goods from a shop. The member of staff was arrested and an investigation is on-going.

While in the office, Tom receives an email from the Head of Human Resources. The email reads as follows:

To:	**All staff**
From:	**Donna Morgan, Head of Human Resources**
Subject:	**Smith & Jones Code of Conduct**

Dear all,

In light of recent events and the damage to Smith & Jones' reputation done by staff members actions outside work, please be aware that the Human Resources department has revised the Smith & Jones Code of Conduct, which I attach to this email.

All staff should read the Code as soon as possible.

Kind regards,

Donna

Matter 3

Tom attends a Money Laundering training session at Smith & Jones.

At the start of the session, the managing partner of the firm, Theo Kojak, explains: 'Thank you all for coming here today. The partners and I think it is vital that all staff receive comprehensive money laundering training and we take the issue very seriously. As you all know, we have recently taken measures to ensure our customer due diligence procedures are comprehensive, clear and available to all staff on the intranet. I'd like to take this opportunity to introduce our new MLRO, Roy Fill, who will be leading the session today'.

Matter 4

One of your clients, Briggs Ltd, has recently approached you regarding their plans for overseas expansion. Briggs Ltd makes water purifiers and has developed a new sealed unit that can operate for over five years with zero maintenance except for occasional cleaning. The product has already won a number of awards and the potential market, particularly in Africa could be substantial.

Dave Turnball, the MD, has approached Smith & Jones for advice over the use of agents in one particular African country to secure Government contracts. The agent claims he has close links with government ministers so should be able to secure the contracts. However, after doing some research, Dave has found out that the agent is known for lavish hospitality and taking ministers on expensive holidays as part of his operational approach.

Matter 5

When Tom was visiting RFT Ltd recently, the Marketing Director asked him if he would pretend to be a potential customer and ring up competitors to see what level of discounts they would give compared to their advertised catalogue rates. Furthermore the Director offered him free use of one of the company's cottages if he did this.

Matter 6

Tom has volunteered to be part of a new Sustainability Committee at Smith & Jones. The committee is tasked with writing and implementing a Sustainability Policy within the firm.

TASK 5 (10 MARKS)

Refer to the Project Scenario and Matters 1 and 5

(a)   Identify and explain the threat to Smith & Jones's audit presented by Morris Haulage Ltd's unpaid fees. State what safeguard should have been put in place to eliminate/mitigate this threat and what should be done if the threat cannot be reduced to an acceptable level.

(b)   Identify and explain THREE ethical principles that could be compromised if Tom accepts the offer from the Director of RFT Ltd. Give TWO safeguards you would expect Smith & Jones to have in place to address the threats faced by Tom and explain what Tom should do.

TASK 6 (10 MARKS)

Refer to the Project Scenario and Matter 2.

(a)   Define operational risk

(b)   What type of risk has Smith & Jones succumbed to?

(c)   Will the Smith & Jones Code of Conduct be a legal document?

(d)   What is the function of a Code of Conduct?

(e)   Could the staff member being investigated for shop lifting be subject to disciplinary procedures from the AAT?

(f)   Identify THREE disciplinary procedures that AAT Student members may be subject to.

TASK 7 (10 MARKS)

Refer to the Project Scenario and Matters 1 and 4.

(a)   Outline the four offences detailed in the UK Bribery Act 2010.

(b)   Explain whether the lunch offered to Tom by Morris Haulage Ltd can be considered a bribe and what action Tom should take.

(c)   Explain what advice should be given to Briggs Ltd in respect of its African expansion.

TASK 8 (10 MARKS)

Refer to the Project Scenario and Matter 3.

(a)   With reference to scenario, explain the meaning of organisational culture being set by the 'tone at the top'

(b)   State TWO instances when customer due diligence procedures must be performed

(c)   If Tom encountered an amount of 14,000 Euros coming into a client bank account that he suspected may be the proceeds of a crime, would he have to report this to the MLRO? What is the monetary limit for money laundering offences?

(d)   What is the difference between a protected and authorised disclosure?

TASK 9 (10 MARKS)

Refer to the Project Scenario and Matter 5.

(a)   What is the definition of sustainable development according to the Bruntland Report?

(b)   Sustainable development aims to strike a balance between what TWO areas?

(c)   Name the TWO categories of environmental impact?

(d)   Name THREE ways in which Smith & Jones could limit its environmental impact

(e)   Can accountants achieve positive change towards a sustainable society?

Section 4

MOCK EXAM ANSWERS

TASK 1

(a)   Money laundering is covered under criminal law:

- Offences are detailed in the Proceeds of Crime Act 2002, The Money Laundering Regulations 2007 and The Terrorism Act 2000

- Breach results in criminal prosecution and, if guilty, fines and imprisonment

(LO 1.2) 2 marks in total: 1 mark – criminal, 1 mark for explanation.

(b)   The role of the CCAB is to provide a forum in which matter affecting the profession can be discussed, and enables the profession to speak with a unified voice in the UK and ROI.

(LO 1.3) 1 mark for explanation.

(c)   (i)   Gemma works in audit which is a statutory regulated function. Statutory regulated functions are audit, insolvency and investment.

Gemma also works in other functions that are not statutory regulated, such as accounts prep and tax.

Statutory regulated means that there are other specific laws relating to that area, for example, the Insolvency Act 1986.

(LO 1.2) 3 marks total – 1 for audit, 1 for tax, 1 for explanation of distinction

(i)   The International Audit and Assurance Standards Board (IAASB), part of IFAC, issues international auditing standards.

The Financial Reporting Council (FRC) then reviews and adapts these if necessary for use in the UK, taking advice from the Audit & Assurance Council.

(LO 1.3) 2 marks total – 1 for IAASB, 1 for FRC

TASK 2

(a)   Professional competence and due care.

> *(LO 1.6) 1 mark; can accept just 'professional competence'*

(b)   There are many ways to perform CPD, including

- structured CPD (training courses, conferences, distance learning with assessment) and

- unstructured CPD (reading professional journals and articles, distance learning without assessment).

> *(LO 1.6) 2 marks total – e.g. 1 for reading professional journals, 1 for external training courses, 1 for distance learning*

(c)   Integrity

> *(LO 2.1) 1 mark*

(d)   Ben should first investigate whether anyone in his firm who is technically competent to undertake the work could either help him or at least check the accuracy of his work.

If this is the case, then the proposed fee should reflect this to ensure all parties have time to do the job properly.

If this is not possible, then Ben should not undertake the task.

> *(LO 2.6, 3.2) 3 marks total – 1 for trying to get additional help/supervision, 1 for implications for fees, 1 for refusing the task if necessary*

(e)   (i)   The decision affects the following ethical principles:

- **Integrity** – Greg should be honest and truthful in all professional business relationships. Knowingly making a misleading or untrue statement would lack integrity

- **Professional behaviour** – making a false statement could discredit both Greg's reputation and the reputation of the profession

In addition Greg should consider the Fraud Act 2006:

- By making any representation that he knows to be untrue or misleading, Greg could be guilty of **fraud by misrepresentation**.

> *(LO 2.1, 2.6) 3 marks total – 1 for integrity, 1 for professional behaviour, 1 for fraud by misrepresentation*

(ii)   If Greg has serious doubts over the accuracy or truthfulness of anything he writes in the reference, then should not write it.

> *(LO 2.6) 1 mark for refusing to write it.*

(iii)   Yes, although whether it would be accepted as a defence in court cannot be assumed.

> *(LO 2.6) 1 mark for yes.*

TASK 3

(a)   Yes, Bob can advise the client that Mel, Smith and Co is able to accept the cheque and pay HMRC when the tax becomes due.

> *(LO 2.4) 1 mark – yes.*

(b)   There are various procedures to follow when handling client monies such as this:

- The money must be banked in a separate interest bearing bank account (interest bearing only if the client money is over £2000 and or held for over 2 months)

- Tell the bank what the account is for (for example, 'holding client monies')

- Bank the money in ASAP

- Only release the money when instructed to do so by the client or as previously agreed (for example, pay tax when it becomes due)

- Keep proper records and send the client an annual statement

- Note: You cannot hold investment business's money unless you are FCA regulated

> *(LO 2.4) 2 marks total – 1 for any of handling clients money measures, e.g., put in an interest bearing account if held for over 2 months*

(c)   Not following the correct procedures for handling client money could result in:

- Action by a professional body (e.g. the AAT)

- Legal action taken by the client for breach of contract

- Money laundering charges

- Breach of the investment business rules

- Fraud charges

- Theft charges

> *(LO 2.4) 2 marks total – 1 for: action by professional body, breach of contract/trust, ML, breach of investment rules, fraud, theft.*

TASK 4

(a)   There are three situations in which you can breach confidentiality:

- With written authorisation from the client

- If you have a legal right or duty to do so

- In the public interest (with certain stipulations. For example, ensure you have all the facts; disclosure must be made in good faith to an appropriate authority; seek legal advice first)

> *(LO 2.5) 3 marks total – 1 for written authorisation from client, 1 for legal right/duty, 1 for in the public interest*

(b)   Roger may have breached rules set out by the AAT (or other professional body), his firm's internal procedures and the government (Data Protection Act)

> *(LO 2.3 , 2.5) 3 marks total – 1 for AAT/professional body, 1 for firm's internal procedures, 1 for the government/Data Protection Act*

TASK 5

(a)   This is a self-interest threat.

Smith & Jones may be concerned about not receiving the fees if they do anything to upset Morris Haulage Ltd, such as, for example, issue a bad audit report. This will therefore affect Smith & Jones' objectivity.

The outstanding fees should be paid before the current audit continues. If the fees are not paid, Smith & Jones should cease to act for Morris Haulage Co Ltd.

(LO 2.1) 4 marks total – 1 mark – self interest threat, 1 mark explain, 1 mark for fees should be paid before the audit continues, 1 mark for if not paid audit should not continue until paid.

(b)   The ethical principles involved are as follows:

- **Integrity** – pretending to be a customer to mislead a competitor would be dishonest

- **Objectivity** – free use of the cottage could be viewed as putting Tom under too much influence to agree to the client's requests

- **Professional behaviour** – if Tom's actions became known, they would discredit both his and the profession's reputation.

Safeguards could include the following:

- Written policies on receiving gifts or hospitality from clients – e.g. with financial limits and the policy to have to report all gifts and hospitality to the firm's partners

- Disciplinary procedures for ethical breaches

- Ethics and conduct programmes and training

Tom should decline both the request to impersonate a customer and the free use of the cottage.

(LO 2.1) 6 marks total – 1 mark for each correct principle – integrity, objectivity, professional behaviour. 1 mark for each safeguard. 1 mark for advice to decline offers.

TASK 6

(a)   Operational risk can be defined as 'the risk of losses resulting from inadequate or failed internal processes, people and systems, or external events'.

(LO 1.5) 2 marks total – for correct definition

(b)   The scenario notes that Smith & Jones' reputation has been damaged. Therefore they have succumbed to Reputational Risk.

(LO 1.5) 1 mark – reputational risk

(c)   Smith & Jones Code of Conduct will not be a legal document (such as a contract or a law)

(LO 1.4) 1 mark – no

(d)   The function of a Code of Conduct is twofold: primarily it is to promote good behaviour, but it also serves to hold to account those that do not follow the code.

(LO 1.4) 2 marks – 1 per point

(e)   Yes, the staff member accused of shop lifting could be disciplined by the AAT.

> *(LO 1.2) 1 mark – yes*

(f)   The AAT has a range of disciplinary procedures as laid out in the AAT Disciplinary Regulations. Procedures vary for full/fellow members and student/affiliate members. Procedures for student/affiliate members include:

- Be declared unfit to become a full member

- Have your student registration withdrawn

- Be (severely) reprimanded

- Be fined

- Be debarred from sitting AAT assessments for a period of time

- Have an AAT assessment result declared null & void

- Be required to submit a written undertaking to refrain from continuing or repeating the misconduct in question

> *(LO 1.2) 3 marks – 1 mark for: reprimanded, excluded from membership, suspended etc.*

TASK 7

(a)   The Bribery Act 2010 creates four offences:

- Bribing a person to induce or reward them to perform a relevant function improperly.

- Requesting, accepting or receiving a bribe as a reward for performing a relevant function improperly.

- Using a bribe to influence a foreign official to gain a business advantage.

- A new form of corporate liability for failing to prevent bribery on behalf of a commercial organisation.

> *(LO 2.2) 4 marks total – 1 for each offence*

(b)   Generally speaking, small offers such as lunch cannot be considered a bribe, due to the insignificant amount involved. Tom should therefore accept the lunch.

Polices do vary from firm to firm, but often auditors will have to complete a hospitality register or inform the audit partner in such cases.

> *(LO 2.2) 2 marks total – 1 for not a bribe if explained, 1 for hospitality register or inform the audit partner*

(c)   Even though the agent would not be an employee, Briggs Ltd could still be found guilty of bribery under the UK act for failing to prevent bribery by the agent.

The lavish holidays and entertaining could be viewed as attempts to bribe the government ministers, so Briggs has a risk exposure here. Ignorance is no defence.

For a commercial organisation, it is a defence to have in place 'adequate procedures' to prevent bribery.

Briggs Ltd should be advised to investigate further how the government concerned views such entertainment and whether they breach any local laws or regulations.

It should also be advised to implement robust anti-bribery procedures and even consider using a different agent or approaching relevant ministers directly.

> *(LO 2.2 and 3.5) 4 marks total – 1 for offence of failing to prevent bribery, 1 for agent not an employee, 1 for adequate procedures, 1 for advice*

TASK 8

(a) 'Tone at the top' means that organisational culture ('the way we do things round here') is in large part set by the attitudes and communications of the leaders and managers of an organisation.

At Smith & Jones, Theo Kojak says 'it is vital that all staff receive comprehensive money laundering training and we take the issue very seriously'. He is shifting the culture of the organisation towards this viewpoint.

> *(LO 1.4) 2 marks total – 1 for explaining, 1 for reference to Theo Kojak.*

(b) Customer Due Diligence (CDD) procedures should be carried out in the following situations:

- When establishing a new business relationship

- When carrying out a large occasional transaction (> €15,000)

- When there is suspicion of money laundering or terrorist financing

- When there are doubts about previously obtained customer identification information

- At regular intervals existing clients on a risk sensitive basis

> *(LO 1.5) 2 marks total – 1 for any of: before providing services, new business relationship, large occasional transaction €15,000, suspicion of ML, doubts over previous CDD, regularly on a risk sensitive basis.*

(c) Yes he would have to report this to the MLRO (or SOCA if the firm has no MLRO). There is no de minimis limit for money laundering offences. Note that the 15,000 euro limit relates to the need to perform customer due diligence procedures if there are large occasional transactions. Ensure you understand this distinction and do not get the two confused!

> *(LO 1.5) 2 marks total – 1 mark for yes would have to report, 1 mark for no de minimis limit*

(d) A protected disclosure is a report made by anyone to an MLRO/SOCA by someone who suspects money laundering or terrorist financing. An authorised disclosure is a report made by anyone to an MLRO/SOCA when the person making the report realises they may have been engaged or are about to be engaged in money laundering. Making an authorised disclosure may provide a defence against money laundering charges provided the disclosure was made as soon as possible and reasons for the delay can be demonstrated.

> *(LO 3.4) 3 marks total – 1 for protected is by anyone on suspicion of ML, 2 for authorised is by anyone involved in or about to be involved in ML or who has been involved but in good faith*

TASK 9

(a)   Sustainable development is development (economic growth) that meets the needs of the present without compromising the ability of future generations to meet their own needs.

> *(LO 4.1) 2 marks total – for correct definition – current v future*

(b)   Sustainable development aims to balance increasing economic growth whilst minimising damage to the environment.

> *(LO 4.1) 2 marks total – economic growth balanced with minimal environmental damage.*

(c)   The environment is generally impacted in one of two ways.

-   Firstly, through the use of resources (e.g. deforestation through the use of trees for timber, mining through the use of metals etc.).

-   Secondly, through pollution (e.g. rubbish, carbon emissions).

> *(LO 4.1) 2 marks total – 1 mark for use of resources, 1 mark for pollution*

(d)   There are a number of ways in which Smith & Jones could limit its environmental impact.

It can reduce its use of resources or reduce its levels of pollution.

Measures could be reducing the use of paper, increasing the thermal efficiency of its buildings thus reducing its electricity demands, encouraging staff to cycle to work or using recycled materials where possible.

> *(LO 4.2) 3 marks total – 1 for any practical point, e.g. reduce paper consumption, use of scanning, email, better buildings etc.*

(e)   Yes, accountants can achieve a positive change towards a sustainable society. Accountants often hold senior positions in organisations and can thus influence policies. Accountants also have a duty to act in the public interest and therefore a duty to promote sustainability.

> *(LO 4.2) 1 mark – yes.*